MW01136613

LOVE

AND

WINE

ALEX DIAZ

FOR MY PARENTS AND MY SISTER.
THANK YOU FOR LOVING ME UNCONDITIONALLY.

I LOVE YOU :)

"WE ARE ALL MORTAL
UNTIL THE FIRST KISS
AND THE SECOND GLASS OF WINE."

—EDUARDO GALEANO (1940-2015)

ALSO BY ALEX DIAZ

In the Books

Love and Wine

If is true
and we all have
a guardian angel,
I would give
mine to her
to protect
the guardian angel
protecting her.

She didn't need a dress
to be a princess.
She didn't need a crown
to be a queen.
She didn't need a gentleman
to be a lady.
All she needed was herself
to be a princess,
a queen,
and a lady.

There are going to be
plenty of ones—
the one you loved,
the one you never loved,
the one who loved you,
the one who never loved you—
and through
a handful of ones,
you will find
the one.

When she smiled,
I wondered,
"how in the world
has the world
not fallen in love
with her?"

We kissed
inside a library,
and all the love stories
began to blush.

There are no
winners or losers
in the game
of love—
just those who play
and those who love.

I never asked
for perfect—
I asked
for someone
who would just try—
but I guess
that was too much
to ask.

Every love—
good or bad—
will lead you to
the love of your life.

Her freckles
were imperfections
reminding me
how perfect
this imperfect world
can be.

She didn't realize
how beautiful
her life could be
until she decided
to follow
her dreams.

She believed she could, so she did.
(Proverbs 31:25)

He was convinced
"perfect"
was a person,
and he realized
he was right
when he saw
his future wife
walking towards him
wearing white.

"Careful,"
said his mother,
"don't confuse
the love of your life
with the love
of your youth."

If I were a cat,
I would spend
all my lives
searching
for you.

To social media,
she was boring,
but to life,
she was a carnival
of festivities.

A night sky
filled with stars
worked as a mirror
to her eyes.

Yesterday
you were beautiful—
so very beautiful—
I held you
in my dreams.
Today
you are beautiful—
so very beautiful—
I hold you
in my heart.
Tomorrow
you will be beautiful—
so very beautiful—
I will hold you
in my arms.
You are yesterday,
today,
and forever,
beautiful—
so very beautiful.

-Unborn children

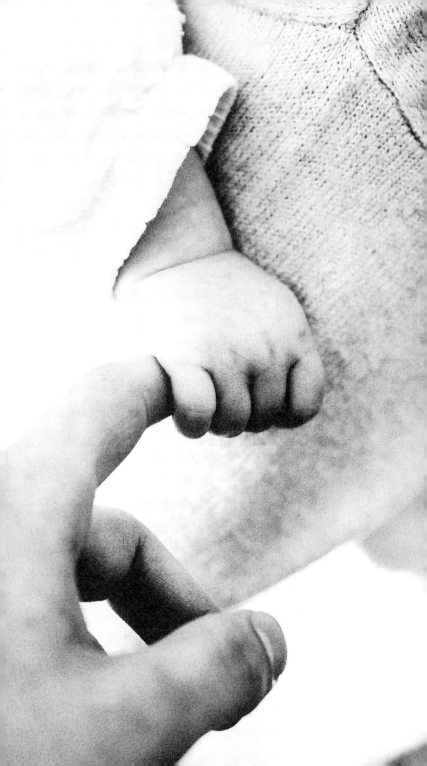

Honey,
your dreams
are your wings—
spread them high
and simply fly.

We kissed at the edge of the park.
She wore an elegant dress.
I wore my father's tux.
It was past curfew,
but we didn't care.
We weren't rebellious—
we were just two kids
falling in love.

At a cafe,
hundreds of miles away,
she told me about her day,
and it felt like a ray

of home.

The best love stories
have an iconic
kissing scene—
can we make sure ours
is no exception?

I hope one day
I can prove
the hypothesis of love
God placed in my heart.

Age
is just a number,
but it does matter—
if we would have met
a few candles sooner,
we would have spent
the rest of our birthdays
together.

She didn't know
when exactly
she stopped living,
but kissing him
brought her life.

"What is something
you would change
about me?"
Nothing.
"Please tell me."
I just did.
"I won't get upset. I promise."
Nothing.
"Please?"
Okay.
I would change
your eyes to mine,
so you could see yourself
the way I do.

You are a galaxy—
fall in love
with all your stars.

Trade
your age
for love,
and you
will be
forever
young.

How ironic—
I gave you my heart,
but I never felt more alone
than the day you decided
to give it back.

I wonder
how many love stories
have never been written
because both characters
were too shy
to smile and say
"hi."

I see you.

I like you.

I lose you.

I miss you.

I forget you.

I love you.

In that order.

She had
one of those smiles
for a smile
smiles—
a smile
you can't help but to smile
when smiled.

When I was in first grade,
I read a fairytale
about dreams coming true
when you wish upon
a shooting star.
After school, I went home,
and waited patiently by the window
in hopes of seeing
one of these stars.
Decades later,
together,
her and I,
saw a shooting star,
and at that moment, I knew,
the fairytale I read in first grade
was based
on a true story.

Ours.

In an age of "sex"—
in an era of "lust"—
choose to be the rare ones
who fall in love.

She looked lovely wearing makeup—
she looked breathtaking wearing freckles.

"Is she hot?"

She's beautiful.

"Did she go home with you?"

None of your business.

"From one to ten?"

Wow, I need new friends.

"Well?"

"I'm sorry, what?" I say.

-College

Mondays with her
are more exciting,
more thrilling,
than weekends
with anyone else.

Never belittle
the colorful beauty
that comes
with brown eyes.

Let us kiss
like in movies—
let us love
like in books—
or let us do both
like in diaries.

What do you say
we get naked?
Keep your clothes on,
but take your fears off.

Girls
fall in love
with fancy.
Women
fall in love
with commitment.

Boys
fall in love
with appearance.
Men
fall in love
with different.

Or is it
the other way around?

She was a young lady
with the fashion
of the '60s,
the romance
of the '70s,
the crazy
of the '80s,
the fun
of the '90s,
and everything good
since then.

I'm not picky—

I just feel cupid is greedy with his arrows.

The heartbroken
play it safe
and choose
not to love
to not get hurt again,
but is it worth
trading a life without love
for a heart without scars?

I promise
I didn't lose
my feelings
towards you—
I just don't know
where they ran off to.

Love
is not a noun.
Stop seeing love
as a person,
place,
thing,
or idea,
and start seeing love
for what it is.

A verb.

She was so broken—
yet, she didn't want a boy
with tape and glue
to put her pieces
back together—
she wanted a man
to find beauty
in all
her broken pieces.

I aspire

my grandchildren

one day

to say

"I want to find a love

like the one

my grandparents have."

All I want

is a dinner

with a good view—

sharing stories

of our childhood.

All I want

is a walk on the beach

with shoes in hand—

enjoying

the warm sand.

All I want

is a long drive

with the windows down—

feeling the wind,

picking songs

we could loudly sing.

All I want

is to enjoy

the joy

of your presence

one

last

time.

-I miss you

He liked books—
she liked movies.
He liked water—
she liked wine.
He liked quiet nights—
she liked late nights.
They had nothing in common,
yet, they always seemed to adored
everything
about their nothing.

She was an unwritten poem
ready to be written.
She felt so much,
but always kept her emotions hidden.
She knew her patience was a virtue,
but she was tired of waiting.
She was worthy of love,
yet, she didn't know
where to start.
Thus, sadly,
she left the piece of paper
blank.

-Unwritten poem

After all this time,
I still can't help
but to be in love
with all the "what ifs"
between us.

She never flirted with men—
she flirted with life—
and for such reason
she was never single.

Honey,
let's share compliments
and pizza slices.

She was
as gentle as a rose,
as delicate as a daisy,
as warm as a sunflower,
and more beautiful
than any flower.

Honey,
gather all the phone numbers you want—
you know mine
by memory anyway.

Most of my childhood
has gone out of business—
and maturely,
so has my love
towards you.

We never had sex,
but to this day,
you're my favorite lover.
You touched my mind and heart
like no other.

You are more than a catch—
you are a game-winning shot
at the last second.

"Why do you love me?"

Because you care for others.

"That's it?"

Because you inspire me.

"That's it?"

Because of the way you smile when you're nervous.

"That's it?"

Because you're beautiful in every way.

"That's it?"

Sweetheart, you're not a "that's it,"

you're my "everything."

You can't spell "princess"
without "prince"—
good thing she wasn't a princess,
but a queen.

She loved herself too much
to allow the opinions of others
to change who she was.

The light of the moon
failed in comparison
to the light
of her soul.

I wanted
to give you my all,
but I'm still waiting
to regain parts of me
given away
in the past.

I'm sorry.

She was more
than the average girl—
she was a diamond
surrounded by pearls.

There was never any crave
to see her undressed,
but a curiosity of her innocence
will forever
remain.

Kissing

is

time

well

spent.

I don't miss
your smile,
your laugh,
or even your love,
but I do miss my life
before it was introduced
to your smile,
your laugh,
and your love.

She turned the "mystery"
in "tomorrow's a mystery"
into a "blessing."
For every day with her
served as a reminder
of how blessed
she was to have her.

"You fool,
don't spend your life
trying to be
good enough
for her—
instead,
spend your life
being good to her."

I still care for you,
but I forgot you
a long time ago.

In a world of common sense, she was a miracle.

Her imperfections
were the best part
of her perfect.

"Be careful
not to label him
too soon
as a prince—
many men
are just frogs
looking for
some sort of fling."

Her dress
was the least
of her outfit—
no one
wore a smile
like her.

I'll lend you my heart,
but please,
return it in one piece
when you're done.

She was convinced
she would end up
alone—
she wasn't hard to love,
but she had trouble
falling in love.

"No,"

he said,

"for I will break your heart."

"It's okay,"

she begged,

"not trying will break it too."

"My love,
thank you
for saying "yes"
and becoming
my fiancé.
My love,
thank you
for stating "I do"
and becoming
my wife.
My love,
with all my heart,
thank you
for being my friend
and blessing
my life."

"Follow me,"
she said,
"for I have years to show you
before the night ends."

Her favorite hobby

was to

tiptoe

towards the lips

of her boyfriend.

Like a holiday ornament,
your memory
hangs freely
for a short season—
before being put away
and forgotten
for a longer season.

There are several
levels of love,
and sometimes
the first couple
are heartbreaks.

His heart
told him
to end things
with her—
now that he has
he wonders
if he
should have argued
with his heart more.

She sang in the shower badly,
her eggs were always undercooked,
she never guessed correctly in charades,
and she was a lousy driver in every way,
yet,
he would never trade
her bad singing,
undercooked eggs,
wrong guesses,
or road rage,
for anything.

Even
if the day we met
would have never taken place,
somehow,
someway,
in another day,
we would have met
and fallen in love
like the first day.

I am sorry for hurting you,

but don't worry,

time has done is thing—

every day without you hurts,

and I guess there's only one soul to blame—

me.

Our love
never made
much sense—
maybe that's why
it felt so real.

I took the road less traveled by
and confessed my dearest dream to her—
she smiled and whispered, "I believe in you,"
and that has made
all the difference
in the world.

I stayed up late last night
watching the weather forecast
to see the probability
of kissing you
in the rain.

Pucker up,
for your best kisses
are yet to come.

Relationships finish—
some lose contact,
some fade away,
some end
before they begin—
I'm glad ours didn't—
you died,
but never left.

-Rest in peace

As the days pass
and the years go by,
remember me.
When you grow older
and overcome life,
remember me.
When thoughts of the past
come to mind,
remember me.
When you're ready to come back,
forget me.

You will fall in love
with a body
millions of times.
You will fall in love
with a mind
thousands of times.
You will fall in love
with a heart
hundreds of times.
You will fall in love
with a soul
once upon a time.

"Women
are a better version
of our equal."

-A man

Her father
broke her heart
way before
any boy
ever could.

Life had blessed her with outer beauty—
everywhere she went
she walked with confidence
of who she was.
Life had blessed her with inner beauty—
everywhere she went
she walked with confidence
of who she was becoming.

Oh how sweet is time
for allowing you and I
to live in the same
lifetime.

You're one of a kind.
I still think of you after all this time.
I still remember your laugh
and the joy in your eyes.
I will always care for you,
and I know
you will always care for me too.

Perhaps when we're older,
married,
and both the luckiest two in the world,
we could enjoy a glass of wine
all four of us.

-Forever friends
but never soulmates

She didn't have
any secrets
in her closet—
but she did have
a few skeletons
in her diary.

Sunrises are nice,
but sleeping in
with the one you love
is nicer.

My heart
has either misled me
or must really enjoy
being alone.

Give any woman
an armor
and she becomes
all the knight shining
she needs.

So many men
had failed her
that she became certain
something was wrong with her,
without knowing
her only flaw
was confusing boys
for men.

This might sound odd,
perhaps even cruel,
but I really do enjoy
missing you.

You were the first girl
to see me cry.
I will never forget you.
You will always be
the first girl
to make me cry.

I can't wait
for a wild youth
to lead me to
gentle you.

I don't know
what tomorrow holds,
but I promise
to live every tomorrow
inspired
to see our love story
unfold
to one another.

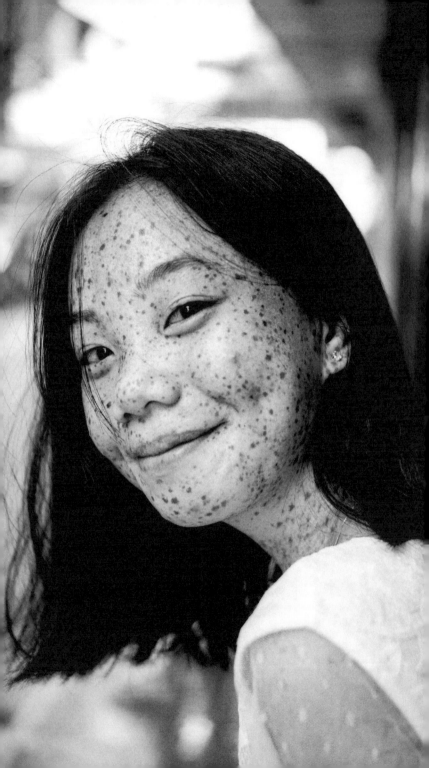

She smiled with timidness,
but loved with fury.

I don't think of you—
I think of the memories.
I still like the memories—
I still don't like you.

Whoever said,
"bad girls don't go to heaven,"
never had the pleasure
of dating one.

If my dearest dream
were a poem,
it would start
with the first letter
of her name,
and it will end
with the last letter
of my last name.

-Wedding day

She was a rare breed of pretty—
the one you admire,
but not desire.

The part of me
that forgot you
loves you
just as much
as the part of me
that didn't forget you.

She didn't realize
the years
she had been
waiting for him
until the second
she decided
to touch his lips.

Thank you, sister,
for you're forever
my dance partner
for life—
thank you
for teaching me
how to dance
on the dance floor
and in life.

She cared for him
too much as a friend
to tell him she loved him
in more ways
than *just friends*.

I love
my future children too much
to not wait patiently
for the best mother
they can have.

-Future wife

I went from missing you
and wanting you to love me,
to missing you
and wanting you to be happy.
I get it now—
you're better off
without me.

Let's face it,
we both deserved better—
let's move on,
but not together.

She made sure
not to confuse
the idea
of loneliness
with the fact
of waiting for
the right soul.

Her mind
challenged me.
Her heart
humbled me.
Her smile
delighted me.
Her love
blessed all of me.

Her charisma
was the "awe"
mumbled
after every told
love story.

Dear soulmate,
what do you say
we break the rules
and meet
a bit
early?

She was guilty
of breaking his heart
to the first degree,
but when it was time to confess,
he begged for her innocence
with all his broken pieces.

"They are beautiful on the outside—
breathtaking on the inside.
Please surround them with angels.
Protect them from harm.
Bless them with love.
Allow them to pursue their dreams
and become everything they want.
Bless their souls
and the souls of those they care for the most.
They are special individuals
I can't help
but to be grateful for."

-Prayers for every woman I've dated

Our first kiss
to forever
will be breathtaking.

-You may kiss the bride

She was bread and butter
to my low-carb diet.

Once upon a time,
he gave
a pretty girl
an empty vase,
so when flowers
were sent,
they would have
a place to rest—
all the flowers
are dead,
but the vase
remains the same,
as she wonders
if he
will ever send
flowers
again.

It was right then and there,
on a red light
of a city street,
where I dared her to kiss me
until the light
turned green.
She kissed me,
our eyes closed,
time stopped,
and I did not go
until I heard a honk
coming from
the car behind.

I wear my heart on my sleeve.

Can we shake hands?

She never had darkness—her faith was her light.

"Remember,"
her father once told him,
"protect my daughter
for she is yours,
but love my daughter
for she is *hers*
first."

She didn't dream
of an "I love you"—
she dreamt
of an "I love you too."

Thank you
for rejecting me—
you made me realize
I was too good
for you anyway.

She never enjoyed
sports
very much,
yet, she knew,
the most dangerous sport
was falling in love.

His
heartbeat
danced
faster
and faster
with every song
they slow danced to.

She never cared
what color shade
the box of crayons
life gave—
she chose
to colored her life
freely and beautifully
by loving every color
as one color.

-Equality

I know

"we"

will fail,

but I still want

"us"

to try.

He was the verb
that gave
her life sentence
meaning.

I'm tired of words. Lets go make poetry.

She was
as soothing as jazz,
but she was
as tough
as rock-n-roll.

We pay
the overpriced cup
of coffee,
and settle for
the cheap cup
of love.

She loved to dance—
on the dance floor
and on my mind.

The second
I started
loving myself,
was the second
I realized
you
never loved me.

Their parents didn't want them together.
She was starting her career.
He was following his dreams.
But they were in love.
So they loved.
And loved.
And loved.
Until they realized
their parents
were right.

Her broken smile
could glue souls together.

She wanted
the friend between them
to evaporate
in the steam
of a first kiss.

She was tough like a leather jacket,
and classy like one too.

From time to time,
you come to mind,
and I can't help
but to smile—
not because I miss you,
but because I realize
I did it—
I got over you.

I've never enjoyed
the act
of drinking,
but I've always enjoyed
the art
of being drunk
of her.

"Thousands of years have passed,
endless souls have lived and died,
and not one
has been able to describe
love.
The old
are too young
to have experienced
more than an ounce,
more than a drop,
of the ocean
that is *love.*
But there I go
pretending I know
like everyone else
what *love*
truly is.
Maybe *love*
is not a question
we can answer—
maybe *love*
is the answer
to all the questions
we can't answer."

If I were a poet,
I would write a book
filled with poems and stories
for the purpose of hoping
she
would attend my book signing
so I could whisper,
"thank you
for being
the poet
in me."

You.
Yes, you.
You are beautiful,
and the world
is a better place
with you.

Yes, you <3